LIKE AN OAK

PHILIP MASTERSON

Published by

OWL®
PUBLISHERS

www.owlpublishers.com
360 S Market St, San Jose, CA 95113,
United States.

Printed in the United States of America

DEDICATION

I want to dedicate this book to my incredible son, Nathan Masterson. The greatest days of my life were the day you were born, and the day you received the love of God and celebrated by being baptized, lowered into the water, and raised again into a new form, living through faith and remaining gold in the spirit of your youth. In addition, thank you to all the people who have been the light upon my path in life.

How do I become strong?

Like an Oak.

How do I endure the storms of life?

Like an Oak.

How do I trust God?

Like an Oak.

As I grow, how do I remain firm in who I am?

Like an Oak.

For a tree to grow,
a seed must be planted beneath the surface.

Like an Oak.

Beginning as an acorn, only to grow in time
to bloom into something even greater.

Like an Oak.

The seed of life is instilled within to allow new growth.

Like an Oak.

We must nurture the seed with love and peace, protect the seed through obedience, water the seed with faith, and nourish it with gratitude.

Developing deep roots to provide a firm foundation!

Like an Oak.

Becoming the gift of durability.

Like an Oak.

Constructing the gift of adaptability.

Like an Oak.

Building the gift of longevity.

Like an Oak.

I want to produce good fruit.

Like an Oak.

My roots will be anchored in peace, joy, kindness, goodness, gentleness, self-control, patience, and love.

I will grow and strengthen each day through all types of weather.

Like an Oak.

I will reach my limbs wide and change the world.

Like an Oak.

I will triumph in the seasons of difficulty and seasons of sunshine.

Like an Oak.

Are you ready to strengthen from the inside and out?

Like an Oak.

I want the seed to be planted so I may become...

Like an Oak.

Living at peace, knowing God loves me!

Like an Oak.

....to all who believed in him and accepted him as their own, he gave the right to become children of God.

John 1:12 NLT

If you are ready for the seed of Christ to be planted, say, "Lord Jesus, thank you for your sacrifice on the cross. I repent of my sins. I ask you to be my Lord and Savior. I entrust my life to your power and guidance through the Holy Spirit. Come into my heart and create me anew. Amen"

Go and be baptized in the water, before many, to celebrate the new birth of the Spirit!

If love never fails, we should never fail to grow in our love for the one who created us!

Like An Oak.

ABOUT THE AUTHOR

Philip Masterson is an author of Christian books
who is inspired to spread the good news to the world.
He developed a passion for God through seeking Him with all
his heart. When he is not writing, he enjoys reading, playing
sports, traveling, and attending church. Dive into another one
of his works, the book Love Pulse, about your love
relationship with God.

www.ingramcontent.com/pod-product-compliance
Lightning Source LLC
Chambersburg PA
CBHW042011080426
42734CB00002B/41